NOAH WEBSTER

& HIS WORDS

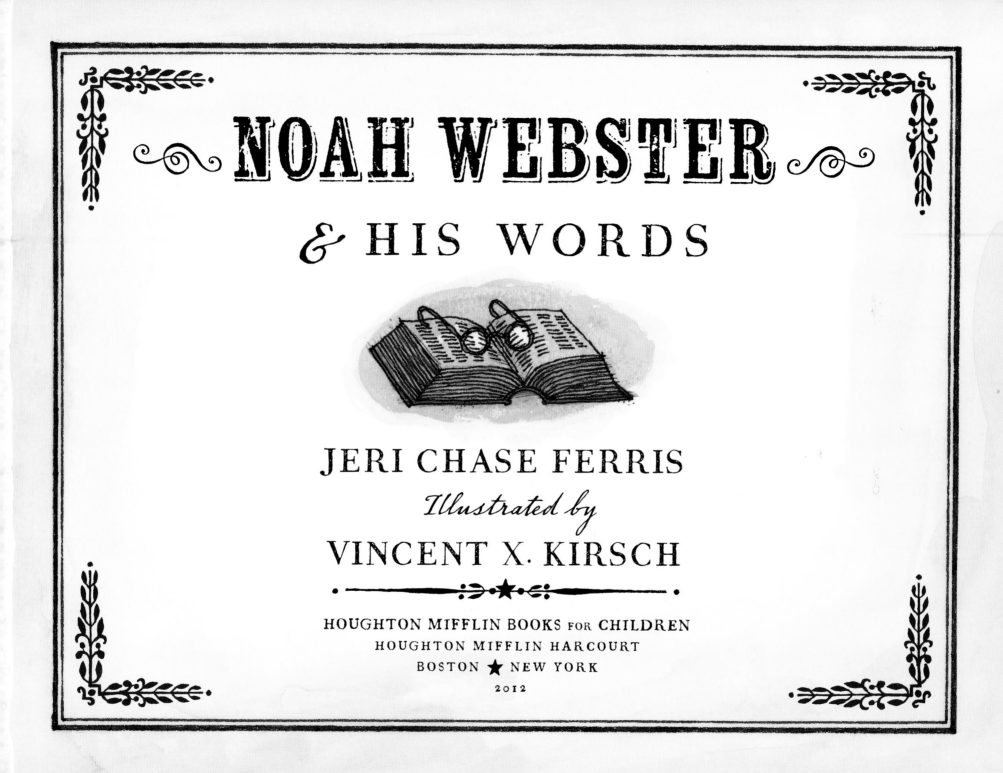

JERI CHASE FERRIS

Illustrated by

VINCENT X. KIRSCH

HOUGHTON MIFFLIN BOOKS FOR CHILDREN
HOUGHTON MIFFLIN HARCOURT
BOSTON ★ NEW YORK
2012

For my sons, Tom and Mark, who always know the right words — J.C.F.

To Kathy Milne, who has a way with words —V.X.K.

Word definitions courtesy of *Webster's New Collegiate Dictionary,* ninth edition, 1985.
All rights reserved. For information about permission to reproduce selections from this book, write to Permissions,
Houghton Mifflin Harcourt Publishing Company, 215 Park Avenue South, New York, New York 10003.
Houghton Mifflin Books for Children is an imprint of Houghton Mifflin Harcourt Publishing Company.

www.hmhbooks.com

The text of this book is set in P22 1722.
The illustrations were made with ink, watercolor, and graphite. And love.

Library of Congress Cataloging-in-Publication Data
Ferris, Jeri.
Noah Webster and his words / by Jeri Chase Ferris ; illustrated by Vincent X. Kirsch.
p. cm. — (Houghton Mifflin Books for children)
ISBN 978-0-547-39055-0
1. Webster, Noah, 1758–1843–Juvenile literature. 2. Lexicographers–United States–Biography–Juvenile literature.
3. Educators–United States–Biography–Juvenile literature. I. Kirsch, Vincent X., ill. II. Title. III. Series.

PE64.W5F47 2012
423'.028092—dc22
[B]
2011013018

Manufactured in China
SCP 10 9 8 7 6 5 4 3 2 1
4500369726

ACKNOWLEDGMENTS:
Christopher I. Dobbs, executive director, Noah Webster House and West Hartford Historical Society: thank you for
your time, your suggestions, and your critical corrections. My critique groups, a source of constant encouragement.
And Kate O'Sullivan, my amazing editor. Noah would be proud!

Noah Webster always knew he was right, and he never got tired of saying so (even if, sometimes, he wasn't). He was, he said, "full of CON-FI-DENCE" [noun: belief that one is right] from the very beginning.

He was born in 1758 on a farm in West Hartford, Connecticut, when America still belonged to England, and by the time he was twelve he knew how to grow everything from beans and corn to peas and potatoes. His father said Noah would be a fine farmer, following in the footsteps of a long line of Webster farmers.

But Noah did not want to be in that long line. He didn't want to be a farmer at all.

Noah wanted to be a SCHOL-AR [noun: one who goes to school; a person who knows a lot]. He wanted to study Latin and Greek. His father said he could — if he did all his work on the farm, too. It wasn't long before Noah's father found him with his nose in a book and his work not done. Red-haired Noah was red-faced with EM-BAR-RASS-MENT [noun: shame; confusion].

Mr. Webster went to see Noah's teacher, the Reverend Perkins. Rev. Perkins CON·VINCED [verb: overcame by argument] Mr. Webster that Noah should be in school, not on the farm. So, when Noah was fifteen, he entered Yale, one of the best colleges in the country. There was only one problem: Yale was EX·PEN·SIVE [adj.: having a high price; costly]. Mr. Webster got a loan on the farm to pay the bill. Noah promised to pay him back.

When Noah graduated from Yale in 1778, the Revolutionary War, which had started in 1775, was still going on. What should he do? Join the army? Study law? Return to farming? He owed his father a lot of money, and he had to get a job fast. He decided he knew enough to be a good teacher.

That fall, Mr. Noah Webster, age nineteen, began teaching school. Like many teachers then, he had no blackboard, no chalk, no pencils or maps. He did have lots of students and a few old schoolbooks from England. But Noah wanted to teach his students about America — he wanted *American* schoolbooks.

In October 1781, King George's soldiers SUR-REN-DERED [**verb:** gave up] at Yorktown. The war was over at last! America was free and IN-DE-PEN-DENT [**adj.:** not controlled by others]. That gave Noah an idea. He would write the schoolbooks for America, beginning with spelling. "I will write the second Declaration of Independence," Noah wrote to a friend. "An American spelling book!"

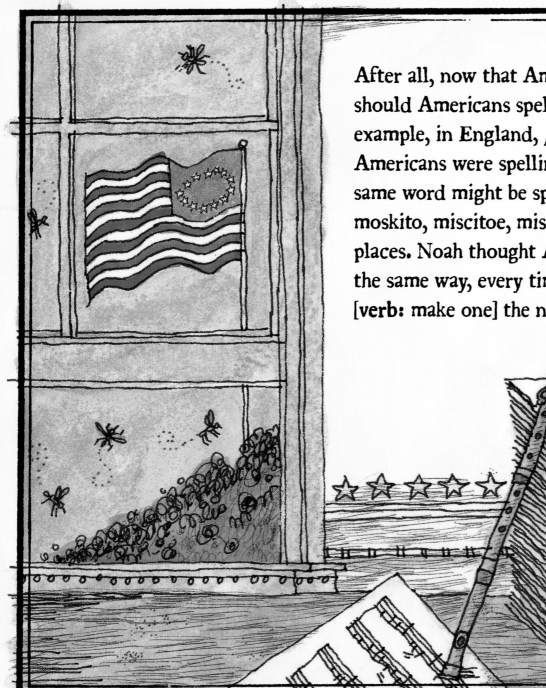

After all, now that America was free from England, why should Americans spell the way they did in England? (For example, in England, *plow* was spelled "plough.") Also, Americans were spelling words any way they wanted, so the same word might be spelled ten different ways (mosquito, moskito, miscitoe, misqutor, muskeetor . . .) in ten different places. Noah thought Americans should spell every word the same way, every time, everywhere. This would U-NITE [**verb:** make one] the new United States.

For almost two years, Noah taught all day and worked on his speller every night. When the book was finished, the PUB-LISH-ER [**noun:** one who prints an author's work] of the *Connecticut Courant* newspaper printed it. Noah wanted his new spelling book to look different from other books on the shelves, so he told his printers to put a blue cover on it. That way, people could just ask for the "blue-backed speller."

The speller cost a lot — fourteen cents — but it SOARED [verb: flew] off the shelves like an American eagle. Noah's book not only taught spelling, but also listed important American dates, towns, and states. At last, in 1783, an American schoolbook!

Noah was very happy with his book, but he still had little money, because he only received one penny for each copy sold. (The printer got the rest.) In 1784 his second book was published, a GRAM-MAR [**noun:** study of words; rules for using words] book.

In 1785 his third book was published, a reading book. The printers were getting rich. Noah was not.

Noah worried about his bills, and he worried about America. There was no president. Each of the thirteen states had its own money and made its own rules. Noah was afraid America would fall into thirteen pieces. "We ought not think of ourselves as people of one state," he wrote, "but as Americans."

He decided to go to every state and talk about his books and his ideas. He went north, south, east, and west. He gave his books to teachers, and he gave LEC-TURES [**noun:** a talk to an audience] to everyone. "*Now* is the time . . . *this* is the country," Noah roared, ". . . let us establish a *national language* [and] government." He liked that part best. He said it as often and as loudly as he could.

In Philadelphia, Noah met Rebecca Greenleaf. He was soon writing in his diary about "the most lovely" Rebecca, and before long they were married. Over the next ten years Noah wrote six more schoolbooks for children and had several children of his own.

He also started a magazine and news-paper so he could tell Americans about their new government. Alas, this turned out to be too much writing — even for Noah Webster.

Noah gave up on the magazine and newspaper business. He settled his family in New Haven, Connecticut, and wrote more schoolbooks. People all over the country were buying his books, especially the "blue-backed speller," and finally Noah had some money.

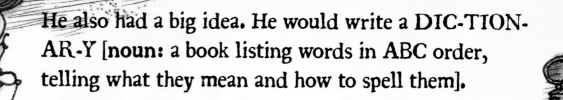

He also had a big idea. He would write a DIC-TION-AR-Y [**noun:** a book listing words in ABC order, telling what they mean and how to spell them].

Two small dictionaries had been printed in America before this, but with English spellings. Noah's dictionary would be 100 percent American — the first American dictionary! He planned to explain every word in the English language, including new American words, such as *skunk, dime,* and *TOM-A-HAWK* [**noun:** an Indian hatchet]. After all, he said, who knew more about American words than Noah Webster?

And, Noah decided, he needed to show where every word in English came from. So he studied twenty different languages, from Arabic to Italian to Welsh. He read almost every book in the local libraries, collecting words for his dictionary. He read almost every book in the Yale University library.

He started his dictionary in 1807, and seventeen years later he was still writing. He needed more books. He needed the great libraries in Paris and London and Cambridge. In 1824 he took his notes and his son William and sailed for Europe.

A year later, with a shaky hand, Noah wrote the meaning of the last word in his dictionary: ZY-GO-MAT-IC [adj.: related to the cheek-bone]. How did it feel to be finished at last? "[It was] difficult to hold my pen steady," he said, "[but after] walking about the room for a few minutes, I recovered."

When Noah and William sailed home to New Haven in June 1826, they were astonished to see crowds of people waiting to greet the author of the first American dictionary. Noah was EC-STAT-IC [adj.: filled with pleasure; delighted; thrilled]!

Now Noah needed to read the two thousand pages he had worked on for almost twenty years, to be sure there were no mistakes.

Next, he needed to find just the right publisher.

Last, he needed to take a nap.

In 1828, when Noah was seventy years old, his *American Dictionary of the English Language* was published. He gave it to America with these words:

To my fellow citizens . . .

for their happiness and learning . . .

for their moral and religious elevation . . .

and for the glory of my country . . .

*N*oah died in 1843 after a long, busy life. But that was not the end of Noah Webster.

When the pioneers went west in the early 1800s, Noah's blue-backed speller was in their covered wagons.

When the Civil War ended in 1865, the newly freed slaves learned to read from Noah's speller.

Noah's dictionary is the second most popular book ever printed in English, after the Bible. It is in every library, in most homes, in our schools, and on our computers—teaching Americans how to spell and use and say nearly every word in the English language.

Noah Webster's
words *did* unite
America. He always
knew he was right!

NOAH WEBSTER AND THE NEW UNITED STATES OF AMERICA

1758 Noah is born in the west division of Hartford, Connecticut, on October 16. This "west division" becomes West Hartford in 1854.

1770 British redcoats (English soldiers) fire on an angry crowd of American COL-O-NISTS [noun: people in one country ruled by another country] in the Boston Massacre.

1777 Noah joins his brothers and their father's militia in a march against British forces, but they don't have to fight.

1778 Noah, age nineteen, graduates from Yale and begins teaching school and studying law.

1781 The British surrender. The Revolutionary War is over.

1783 The Treaty of Paris formally ends the American Revolution. Noah's first book, a speller, is published. He names it *A Grammatical Institute of the English Language*, Part 1. Everyone else calls it "the blue-backed speller."

1784 Noah's second book, a grammar, is published. It is Part 2.

1800 Noah begins work on a small dictionary, which he calls *A Compendious Dictionary of the English Language*. It is published in 1806, but is much too small.

1807 He begins his great American dictionary.

1812 Noah and his family move to Amherst, Massachusetts. He serves in the state legislature and helps found Amherst College. He works on his dictionary.

1822 Noah and his family move to New Haven to be closer to the Yale libraries. He works on his dictionary.

1824 Noah sails to Europe to use the libraries in France and England for his dictionary.

1773 The colonists become angrier over the rules made for them by their king in England. On December 16 there is an uprising—called the Boston Tea Party—against British taxation without representation (Americans must pay taxes to England but have no vote in England).

1774 Noah, age fifteen, enters Yale in New Haven, Connecticut. (We think Noah's father took out a loan on his farm to pay for Noah's years at Yale, but the actual loan papers have not been found.)

1775 General George Washington rides through New Haven on his way to take command of the brand-new American army. Noah proudly plays his flute in the parade.

1775 American MIN-UTE-MEN [noun: men ready to fight on a minute's notice] battle British redcoats at Lexington and Concord. The American Revolution begins.

1776 The Declaration of Independence is signed on July 4.

1785 Noah visits George Washington to discuss the need for a strong central government (and to play cards with George and Martha). Noah's third book, a reader, is published (Part 3). He travels the country to promote his books and his ideas.

1787 The Constitution of the United States is RAT-I-FIED [verb: approved] and becomes law. Some of Noah's ideas are in it. Noah moves to New York City and begins to edit the *American Magazine*. It lasts one year.

1789 George Washington becomes the first president of the United States on April 30. In October, Noah marries Rebecca Greenleaf and they move to Hartford, Connecticut. Noah continues to write books, essays, and lectures. He also works as a lawyer.

1793 Noah moves back to New York City and begins publishing a newspaper, the *American Minerva*. It lasts five years.

1798 The Webster family moves to New Haven, Connecticut.

1825 Noah writes the last word in his dictionary, packs his papers, and sails home.

1828 *Webster's Dictionary* is published after twenty years of work. Noah continues to write more books, essays, and lectures.

1843 Noah Webster dies in New Haven and is buried in the Grove Street Cemetery next to Yale University.

More About Noah Webster

Noah Webster loved words. He loved to sing and dance and play the flute, too. He thought he had quite a nice voice, so he taught singing as an added attraction while traveling to promote his books. He went to balls and dances whenever he could, and wrote in his diary that he felt "exceedingly well after dancing." He even met his future wife, Rebecca, while dancing.

Noah and Rebecca had eight children (Emily, Julia, Harriet, Mary, William, Eliza, Henry, and Louisa), and Noah's pockets were always filled with candies and treats. He cared deeply about his children, and about the future of all the children in the new United States of America. "The first job of government is the education of its children," he wrote. And that's what Noah's words were meant to do.

When Noah wasn't singing or dancing or playing the flute, he was probably writing – or talking. As soon as the Revolutionary War was over in 1781, Noah began to talk about the need for one strong central government, not thirteen separate ones. (The new United States did not even have a president until 1789!) He talked to George Washington about the need to have the same laws for the whole country. General Washington talked to James Madison, who was working on the CON-STI-TU-TION [noun: basic laws of a nation], and Mr. Madison thanked Noah for his ideas.

Noah Webster also knew Benjamin Franklin, Alexander Hamilton, Thomas Paine, Charles Willson Peale, Dr. Benjamin Rush, David Rittenhouse, Ezra Stiles, and more. They dined together, talked together, argued together. They built a new nation together.

"Every child in America should be acquainted with his own country," Noah said. So he wrote American history books (in addition to spelling books, reading books, geography books, science books, health books, and the dictionary).

Noah worked for public health and school reform, opposed slavery, pushed for the first COP-Y-RIGHT LAW [noun: legal right to copy and sell an author's work], and was a teacher, a lawyer, a county court judge, a member of the General Assembly of Connecticut and the General Court of Massachusetts, a founder of Amherst College, and more. He loved his country passionately.

Bibliography

PRIMARY SOURCES:

Dobbs, Christopher. Executive director, Noah Webster House. Correspondence, 2009, 2010.

Field, Howard B. Great-great-grandson of Noah Webster. Correspondence, 1984.

Webster, Noah. *Letters of Noah Webster.* Edited by Harry R. Warfel. New York: Library Publishers, 1953.

Webster, Noah. *On Being American: Selected Writings, 1783-1828.* Edited by Homer D. Babbidge, Jr. New York: Frederick A. Praeger, 1967.

SECONDARY SOURCES:

Babbidge, Homer D., Jr. Editor's introduction to *On Being American: Selected Writings, 1783-1828* by Noah Webster, 3-15. New York: Frederick A. Praeger, 1967.

Commager, Henry Steele. Introductory essay to *Noah Webster's American Spelling Book.* New York: Columbia University Press, 1962.

Ford, Emily Ellsworth Fowler (Webster's granddaughter). *Notes on the Life of Noah Webster.* New York: privately printed, 1912.

Malone, Dumas, editor. *Dictionary of American Biography.* New York: Charles Scribner's Sons, 1936.

Monaghan, Jennifer. *A Common Heritage: Webster's Blue-Backed Speller.* Hamden, Conn.: Archon Books, 1983.

Myers, Robin, editor. *A Dictionary of Literature in the English Language.* Oxford, U. K.: Pergamon Press, 1979.

Rollins, Richard. *The Long Journey of Noah Webster.* Philadelphia: University of Pennsylvania Press, 1980.

Slater, Rosalie J. Introductory essay to *Webster's American Dictionary of the English Language.* San Francisco: Foundation for American Christian Education, 1995 (facsimile reproduction of 1828 edition).

Unger, Harlow Giles. *Noah Webster: The Life and Times of an American Patriot.* New York: John Wiley & Sons, 1998.

Warfel, Harry R. *Noah Webster: Schoolmaster to America.* New York: Octagon Books, 1966.

WEBSITES:

www.noahwebsterhouse.org
Be sure to visit the Kid's Corner for special activities.

www.amherst.edu/library/archives/exhibitions/webster

openlibrary.org/authors/OL6821920A/Noah_Webster

The American Spelling Book . . . Being the First Part of a Grammatical Institute of the English Language (familiarly called The Blue-Backed Speller). It is online at sites such as www.library.pitt.edu/libraries/drl